Paleo Gluten-Free Breads

Delicious Recipes for Gluten-Free Muffins, Biscuits, Cakes, and Breads

Disclaimer and Terms of Use:

Effort has been made to ensure that the information in this book is accurate and complete, however, the author and the publisher do not warrant the accuracy of the information, text and graphics contained within the book due to the rapidly changing nature of science, research, known and unknown facts and internet. The Author and the publisher do not hold any responsibility for errors, omissions or contrary interpretation of the subject matter herein. This book is presented solely for motivational and informational purposes only.

Table of Contents

Introduction

When you switch to the Paleo gluten-free diet you may be worried that you will have to give up your favorite foods – including bread. The good news is that you can still enjoy all kinds of bread on the Paleo diet, all you have to do is use different ingredients. Using gluten-free flours like almond flour, coconut flour, and tapioca flour you can make all kinds of breads including muffins, biscuits, cakes, pancakes, waffles, and quick breads. With the right ingredients you can make delicious gluten-free breads that taste like the real thing.

If you are ready to give the Paleo gluten-free diet a try, this book is the perfect place to start. In this book you will find a collection of delicious gluten-free bread recipes for everything from pancakes to cupcakes. These recipes are easy to prepare and full of flavor – what are you waiting for? Grab an apron and start baking!

Paleo Gluten-Free Bread Recipes

Recipes Included in this Book:

Easy Coconut Flour Pancakes

Cinnamon Blueberry Muffins

Coconut Flour Drop Biscuits

Gluten-Free English Muffins

Coconut Flour Waffles

Bacon Cheddar Biscuits

Chocolate Zucchini Muffins

Cinnamon Banana Pancakes

Almond Flour Biscuits

Apple Walnut Muffins

Carob Chip Waffles

Spiced Carrot Cake Muffins

Almond Flour Blueberry Pancakes

Banana Walnut Bread

Easy Coconut Flour Pancakes

Servings: 4

Ingredients:

- 4 large eggs, beaten well
- 1 cup coconut milk
- 1 ½ tablespoons raw honey
- ½ tablespoon vanilla extract
- ½ cup sifted coconut flour
- 1 teaspoon baking soda
- ¼ teaspoon salt

Instructions:

1. Preheat a large nonstick skillet over medium heat.
2. Beat the eggs until frothy in a mixing bowl then whisk in the coconut milk, honey, and vanilla extract.
3. In a separate bowl, whisk together the coconut flour, baking soda and salt.

4. Whisk the wet ingredients into the dry until smooth and lump-free.
5. Spoon the batter into the preheated skillet, using 2 to 3 tablespoons per pancake.
6. Cook the pancakes for 2 to 3 minutes until bubbles form in the surface of the batter.
7. Flip the pancakes and cook for 1 to 2 minutes more until the underside is browned.
8. Slide the pancakes onto a plate and repeat with the remaining batter.

Cinnamon Blueberry Muffins

Servings: 12

Ingredients:

- 2 ¾ cups blanched almond flour
- 2 tablespoons coconut flour
- ¾ teaspoon baking soda
- Pinch salt
- 1/3 cup melted coconut oil
- 1/3 cup unsweetened almond milk
- ¼ cup raw honey
- 2 large eggs, beaten well
- 2 teaspoons vanilla extract
- 1 cup fresh blueberries

Instructions:

1. Preheat the oven to 350°F and line the muffin pan with paper liners.
2. Combine the flours, baking soda and salt in a mixing bowl.

3. In a separate bowl, whisk together the coconut oil, honey, almond milk, eggs, and vanilla extract.
4. Whisk the wet ingredients into the dry until smooth and lump-free.
5. Fold in the blueberries then spoon the batter into the prepared pan, filling the cups ¾ full.
6. Bake for 20 to 25 minutes until a knife inserted in the center comes out clean.

Coconut Flour Biscuits

Servings: 12

Ingredients:

- ½ cup sifted coconut flour
- ½ teaspoon baking powder
- ¼ teaspoon salt
- 1/3 cup coconut oil
- 5 large eggs, beaten well
- 2 tablespoons raw honey

Instructions:

1. Preheat the oven to 400°F and line a baking sheet with parchment.
2. Combine all of the ingredients in a food processor and blend smooth.
3. Divide the dough into twelve small balls and place them on the baking sheet.
4. Flatten the dough balls with a fork to about ½-inch thick.

5. Bake the biscuits for 12 to 15 minutes until lightly browned.

Gluten-Free English Muffins

Servings: 1

Ingredients:

- 2 teaspoons coconut oil
- ¼ teaspoon apple cider vinegar
- Pinch baking soda
- 1 tablespoon coconut flour
- 1 tablespoon coconut milk
- 1 large egg, beaten well
- Pinch salt

Instructions:

1. Melt the coconut oil in a 6-ounce ramekin.
2. Whisk together the vinegar and baking soda in a small bowl – set aside.
3. Combine the remaining ingredients in the ramekin and stir until well combined.

4. Stir in the baking soda mixture then microwave for 1 minute 30 seconds until set.
5. Cool the English muffin then slice in half and toast to serve.

Coconut Flour Waffles

Servings: 4 to 6

Ingredients:

- 8 large eggs, beaten well
- ½ cup melted coconut oil
- 2 teaspoons vanilla extract
- ½ cup sifted coconut flour
- Pinch salt

Instructions:

1. Preheat your waffle iron according to the manufacturer's instructions.
2. Beat the eggs in a large mixing bowl and whisk in the coconut oil and vanilla extract.
3. Whisk together the coconut flour and salt in a separate bowl.
4. Beat the dry ingredients into the wet until smooth and lump-free.

5. Spoon the batter into the preheated waffle iron according to the manufacturer's instructions.
6. Repeat the process with the remaining batter and serve hot drizzled with honey.

Bacon Cheddar Biscuits

Servings: 12 to 16

Ingredients:

- 1 ¾ cups blanched almond flour
- ¼ cup tapioca flour
- 1 teaspoon dry mustard powder
- ½ teaspoon paprika
- Pinch salt
- 2 cups shredded cheddar cheese
- ¼ cup softened coconut oil
- 4 strips cooked bacon, chopped fine

Instructions:

1. Combine the almond flour, tapioca flour, mustard powder, paprika and salt in a bowl.
2. Toss in the shredded cheese then cut in the coconut oil and stir in the bacon.
3. Knead the mixture by hand into a dough, adding extra coconut oil if needed.

4. Roll the dough out into a log and chill for one hour.
5. Preheat the oven to 350°F.
6. Slice the log into ½-inch slices and place them on a parchment-lined baking sheet.
7. Bake for 20 to 22 minutes until the edges are browned.

Chocolate Zucchini Muffins

Servings: 12

Ingredients:

- ½ cup blanched almond flour
- 5 tablespoons coconut flour
- ¼ cup unsweetened cocoa powder
- 1 teaspoon baking soda
- Pinch salt
- ¼ cup melted coconut oil
- ¼ cup raw honey
- ¼ cup unsweetened almond milk
- 4 large eggs, beaten well
- 1 tablespoon vanilla extract
- 1 cup shredded zucchini, squeezed to remove moisture

Instructions:

1. Preheat the oven to 350°F and line the muffin pan with paper liners.
2. Combine the flours, cocoa powder, baking soda and salt in a mixing bowl.
3. In a separate bowl, whisk together the coconut oil, honey, almond milk, eggs, and vanilla extract.
4. Whisk the wet ingredients into the dry until smooth and lump-free.
5. Fold in the zucchini then spoon the batter into the prepared pan, filling the cups ¾ full.
6. Bake for 25 to 30 minutes until a knife inserted in the center comes out clean.

Cinnamon Banana Pancakes

Servings: 4

Ingredients:

- 3 large overripe bananas, peeled and sliced
- 6 large eggs, beaten well
- 1/3 cup sifted coconut flour
- 1 teaspoon ground cinnamon
- Pinch salt

Instructions:

1. Preheat a large nonstick skillet over medium heat.
2. Combine all of the ingredients in a blender and blend smooth.
3. Spoon the batter into the preheated skillet, using 2 to 3 tablespoons per pancake.
4. Cook the pancakes for 2 to 3 minutes until bubbles form in the surface of the batter.
5. Flip the pancakes and cook for 1 to 2 minutes more until the underside is browned.

6. Slide the pancakes onto a plate and repeat with the remaining batter.

Almond Flour Biscuits

Servings: 8

Ingredients:

- 2 cups blanched almond four
- 2 teaspoons baking powder
- 1 teaspoon salt
- 2/3 cup coconut oil
- 8 large egg whites, beaten until frothy

Instructions:

1. Preheat the oven to 350°F and line a baking sheet with parchment.
2. Combine the almond flour, baking powder and salt in a food processor.
3. Pulse to combine then pulse in the coconut oil.
4. Add the egg whites and pulse until the mixture starts to come together.
5. Divide the mixture into eight even-sized pieces and shape them into discs.

6. Place the biscuits on the baking sheet and bake for 22 to 25 minutes until browned.

Apple Walnut Muffins

Servings: 12

Ingredients:

- 2 ¾ cups blanched almond flour
- 2 tablespoons coconut flour
- 1 teaspoon ground cinnamon
- ¾ teaspoon baking soda
- Pinch salt
- 1/3 cup melted coconut oil
- 1/3 cup unsweetened almond milk
- ¼ cup raw honey
- 2 large eggs, beaten well
- 2 teaspoons vanilla extract
- 1 large ripe apple, peeled and diced
- ½ cup chopped walnuts

Instructions:

1. Preheat the oven to 350°F and line the muffin pan with paper liners.

2. Combine the flours, cinnamon, baking soda and salt in a mixing bowl.
3. In a separate bowl, whisk together the coconut oil, honey, almond milk, eggs, and vanilla extract.
4. Whisk the wet ingredients into the dry until smooth and lump-free.
5. Fold in the apples and walnuts then spoon the batter into the prepared pan, filling the cups ¾ full.
6. Bake for 20 to 25 minutes until a knife inserted in the center comes out clean.

Carob Chip Waffles

Servings: 4 to 6

Ingredients:

- 8 large eggs, beaten well
- ½ cup melted coconut oil
- 2 teaspoons vanilla extract
- ½ cup sifted coconut flour
- Pinch salt
- ½ cup mini carob chips

Instructions:

1. Preheat your waffle iron according to the manufacturer's instructions.
2. Beat the eggs in a large mixing bowl and whisk in the coconut oil and vanilla extract.
3. Whisk together the coconut flour and salt in a separate bowl.
4. Beat the dry ingredients into the wet until smooth and lump-free then fold in the carob chips.

5. Spoon the batter into the preheated waffle iron according to the manufacturer's instructions.
6. Repeat the process with the remaining batter and serve hot drizzled with honey.

Spiced Carrot Cake Muffins

Servings: 12

Ingredients:

- 2 cups blanched almond flour
- 1 teaspoon baking soda
- 1 teaspoon ground cinnamon
- ¼ teaspoon ground nutmeg
- Pinch salt
- ½ cup melted coconut oil
- ½ cup raw honey
- 3 large eggs, beaten well
- 1 ½ teaspoons vanilla extract
- 1 cup shredded carrot, squeezed to remove moisture
- ½ cup seedless raisins

Instructions:

1. Preheat the oven to 350°F and line the muffin pan with paper liners.

2. Combine the flour, baking soda, cinnamon, nutmeg and salt in a mixing bowl.
3. In a separate bowl, whisk together the coconut oil, honey, eggs, and vanilla extract.
4. Whisk the wet ingredients into the dry until smooth and lump-free.
5. Fold in the carrots and raisins then spoon the batter into the prepared pan, filling the cups ¾ full.
6. Bake for 18 to 20 minutes until a knife inserted in the center comes out clean.

Almond Flour Blueberry Pancakes

Servings: 4

Ingredients:

- 1 ½ cups blanched almond flour
- 3 large eggs, whisked well
- 1 cup unsweetened almond milk
- Pinch salt
- 1 cup fresh blueberries

Instructions:

1. Preheat a large nonstick skillet over medium heat.
2. Combine all of the ingredients in a large bowl and whisk until smooth and lump-free.
3. Spoon the batter into the preheated skillet, using 2 to 3 tablespoons per pancake.
4. Sprinkle a few blueberries into the wet batter of each pancake.
5. Cook the pancakes for 2 to 3 minutes until bubbles form in the surface of the batter.

6. Flip the pancakes and cook for 1 to 2 minutes more until the underside is browned.
7. Slide the pancakes onto a plate and repeat with the remaining batter.

Banana Walnut Bread

Servings: 8 to 10

Ingredients:

- 4 overripe bananas, peeled and mashed
- 4 large eggs, beaten well
- ½ cup smooth almond butter
- ¼ cup coconut oil
- 1 ½ teaspoons vanilla extract
- ½ cup sifted coconut flour
- 3 teaspoons ground cinnamon
- 1 ¼ teaspoon baking soda
- ¾ teaspoon baking powder
- ¼ teaspoon salt
- ½ cup chopped walnuts

Instructions:

1. Preheat the oven to 350°F and grease a regular loaf pan.

2. Combine the bananas, eggs, almond butter, coconut oil and vanilla in a food processor.
3. Blend the mixture smooth then add the coconut flour, cinnamon, baking soda, baking powder and salt.
4. Pulse the mixture several times to combine then blend smooth.
5. Fold in the walnuts then pour the mixture into the loaf pan and spread it evenly.
6. Bake for 55 to 60 minutes until a knife inserted in the center comes out clean.
7. Cool the bread completely before cutting it into slices.

Gluten-Free Sandwich Bread

Servings: 12 to 15

Ingredients:

- ¾ cup smooth almond butter
- ¼ cup melted coconut oil
- 2 ½ tablespoons raw honey
- 6 large eggs, beaten well
- ¾ teaspoon cider vinegar
- ¼ cup ground flaxseed
- 3 ½ tablespoons coconut flour
- 1 ¼ teaspoon baking soda
- ¼ teaspoon salt

Instructions:

1. Preheat the oven to 350°F and grease a regular loaf pan.
2. Combine the almond butter, coconut oil, honey and eggs in a food processor.

3. Blend the mixture until smooth then add the vinegar – blend well.
4. Combine the dry ingredients in a mixing bowl then blend into the wet ingredients.
5. Pour the batter into the prepared pan and spread it evenly.
6. Bake for 35 to 40 minutes until a knife inserted in the center comes out clean.
7. Cool the bread completely before cutting it into slices.

Spiced Pumpkin Nut Bread

Servings: 8 to 10

Ingredients:

- ½ cup sifted coconut flour
- 1 tablespoon ground cinnamon
- ½ teaspoon ground nutmeg
- Pinch ground cloves
- ½ teaspoon baking soda
- ¼ teaspoon baking powder
- Pinch salt
- 1 cup pumpkin puree
- ½ cup raw honey
- ¼ cup coconut oil
- 1 teaspoon vanilla extract
- 4 large eggs, beaten well
- ½ cup chopped walnuts

Instructions:

1. Preheat the oven to 350°F and grease a regular loaf pan.
2. Combine the dry ingredients in a mixing bowl until well combined.
3. In a separate bowl, whisk together the pumpkin, honey, coconut oil, vanilla and eggs.
4. Whisk the dry ingredients into the wet until smooth and well combined.
5. Fold in the walnuts then pour the batter into the prepared pan.
6. Bake for 45 to 60 minutes until a knife inserted in the center comes out clean.
7. Cool the bread completely before cutting it into slices.

Microwave Sandwich Bread

Servings: 1

Ingredients:

- 1 tablespoon coconut flour
- ¼ teaspoon baking powder
- 1 tablespoon melted coconut oil
- 1 large egg, beaten well

Instructions:

1. Whisk together all of the ingredients in a bowl until smooth.
2. Grease a plastic sandwich container and pour the batter in.
3. Spread the batter then microwave on high for 90 seconds until puffed and set.
4. Slice the bread in half lengthwise and serve.

Cinnamon Zucchini Bread

Servings: 10 to 12

Ingredients:

- ¾ cups blanched coconut flour
- 1 ½ teaspoon ground cinnamon
- 1 teaspoon baking soda
- ½ teaspoon salt
- 6 large eggs, beaten well
- ½ cup raw honey
- ¼ cup melted coconut oil
- 1 ½ teaspoon vanilla extract
- 1 ½ cups shredded zucchini, squeezed to remove moisture

Instructions:

1. Preheat the oven to 350°F and grease a regular loaf pan.
2. Combine the dry ingredients in a mixing bowl until well combined.

3. In a separate bowl, whisk together the eggs, honey, coconut oil and vanilla.
4. Whisk the dry ingredients into the wet until smooth and well combined.
5. Fold in the zucchini then pour the batter into the prepared pan.
6. Bake for 45 to 60 minutes until a knife inserted in the center comes out clean.
7. Cool the bread completely before cutting it into slices.

Herbed Coconut Flour Bread

Servings: 10 to 12

Ingredients:

- 4 large eggs, beaten well
- ¼ cup unsweetened almond milk
- ¼ cup olive oil
- 1 teaspoon fresh chopped rosemary
- ½ teaspoon fresh chopped thyme
- ½ teaspoon fresh chopped oregano
- ¾ cups sifted coconut flour
- 6 tablespoons ground flaxseed
- 1 teaspoon baking soda
- ½ teaspoon salt

Instructions:

1. Preheat the oven to 350°F and grease a regular loaf pan.
2. Beat together the eggs, almond milk, olive oil and herbs until smooth.

3. Add the dry ingredients and whisk until well combined.
4. Pour the batter into the loaf pan and spread evenly.
5. Bake for 45 minutes until a knife inserted in the center comes out clean.
6. Cool the bread completely before slicing to serve.

Cinnamon Raisin Bread

Servings: 10 to 12

Ingredients:

- 1 cup sifted coconut flour
- 6 large eggs, beaten well
- ¾ cups mashed sweet potato
- ¼ cup coconut oil, melted
- 2 tablespoons fresh lemon juice
- 2 teaspoons vanilla extract
- 1 tablespoon ground cinnamon
- 2 teaspoons baking soda
- ¼ teaspoon salt
- 1 cup seeded raisins

Instructions:

1. Preheat the oven to 350°F and grease two mini loaf pans.
2. Combine all of the ingredients except the raisins in a food processor.

3. Blend until smooth then fold in the raisins.
4. Divide the mixture between the two loaf pans and bake for 40 minutes.
5. Cover the loaf pans with foil and bake for another 20 minutes.
6. Cool the loaves completely before slicing to serve.

Chocolate Cupcakes

Servings: 12

Ingredients:

- 6 tablespoons coconut flour
- 6 tablespoons unsweetened cocoa powder
- ½ teaspoon baking soda
- ½ teaspoon salt
- 6 large eggs, beaten well
- ½ cup raw honey
- 1/3 cup coconut oil
- 1 teaspoon vanilla extract

Instructions:

1. Preheat the oven to 350°F and line a muffin pan with paper liners.
2. Combine the coconut flour, cocoa powder, baking soda and salt in a mixing bowl.
3. In a separate bowl, beat together the eggs, honey, coconut oil and vanilla.

4. Whisk the dry ingredients into the wet until smooth then spoon into the prepared pan.
5. Bake for 15 to 18 minutes until a knife inserted in the center comes out clean.
6. Cool the cupcakes completely before frosting.

Cinnamon Pumpkin Sheet Cake

Servings: 10 to 12

Ingredients:

- 1 cup pumpkin puree
- 6 tablespoons pure maple syrup
- ¼ cup melted coconut oil
- 2 large eggs, beaten well
- 1 ½ teaspoon vanilla extract
- 1 ½ cups blanched almond flour
- 1 ½ teaspoon ground cinnamon
- ¾ teaspoon baking powder
- ½ teaspoon ground nutmeg
- ¼ teaspoon salt

Instructions:

1. Preheat the oven to 350°F and grease a square glass baking dish.
2. Whisk together the pumpkin, maple syrup, coconut oil, eggs, and vanilla extract.

3. Combine the remaining ingredients in a mixing bowl until well combined.
4. Whisk the dry ingredients into the wet until smooth.
5. Spread the batter in the prepared pan and bake for 30 to 35 minutes until a knife inserted in the center comes out clean.

Vanilla Cupcakes

Servings: 12

Ingredients:

- ½ cup coconut flour
- ½ teaspoon baking soda
- ¼ teaspoon salt
- 6 large eggs, beaten well
- ½ cup coconut oil
- ¼ cup raw honey
- 1 ½ tablespoons vanilla extract

Instructions:

1. Preheat the oven to 350°F and line a muffin pan with paper liners.
2. Combine the coconut flour, baking soda and salt in a mixing bowl.
3. In a separate bowl, beat together the eggs, honey, coconut oil and vanilla.

4. Whisk the dry ingredients into the wet until smooth then spoon into the prepared pan.
5. Bake for 15 to 18 minutes until a knife inserted in the center comes out clean.
6. Cool the cupcakes completely before frosting.

Easy Paleo Carrot Cake

Servings: 10 to 12

Ingredients:

- ¾ cups sifted coconut flour
- 3 teaspoons ground cinnamon
- ½ teaspoon ground nutmeg
- 1 teaspoon salt
- 10 large eggs, beaten well
- 1 cup melted coconut oil
- 1 cup raw honey
- 1 tablespoon vanilla extract
- 5 large carrots, peeled and shredded

Instructions:

1. Preheat the oven to 325°F and grease a 9x13-inch baking dish with cooking spray.
2. Whisk together the flour, cinnamon, baking soda, nutmeg and salt in a mixing bowl.

3. In a separate bowl, whisk together the eggs, coconut oil, honey and vanilla extract.
4. Stir the dry ingredients into the wet until smooth and well combined then fold in the shredded carrots.
5. Spread the cake batter in the prepared pan and bake for 35 to 45 minutes until a knife inserted in the center comes out clean.

Coconut Cupcakes

Servings: 12

Ingredients:

- ½ cup coconut flour
- ½ teaspoon baking soda
- ¼ teaspoon salt
- 6 large eggs, beaten well
- ½ cup coconut oil
- ¼ cup raw honey
- 1 teaspoon vanilla extract
- ¾ cup shredded unsweetened coconut

Instructions:

1. Preheat the oven to 350°F and line a muffin pan with paper liners.
2. Combine the coconut flour, baking soda and salt in a mixing bowl.
3. In a separate bowl, beat together the eggs, honey, coconut oil and vanilla.

4. Whisk the dry ingredients into the wet until smooth then fold in the coconut.
5. Spoon into the prepared pan.
6. Bake for 15 to 18 minutes until a knife inserted in the center comes out clean.
7. Cool the cupcakes completely before frosting.

Conclusion

Switching to the gluten-free Paleo diet does not necessarily mean giving up all of your favorite foods. Following the gluten-free Paleo diet is a healthy choice, but it doesn't have to be a boring one. With the right ingredients, you can still enjoy everything from muffins and pancakes to quick breads and cupcakes. If you are ready to give the Paleo gluten-free diet a try, this book is the perfect place to start. Just pick a recipe from the collection and get baking!

12231347R00032

Printed in Great Britain
by Amazon